"WHAT THE CHILD IMITATES, HE BEGINS TO UNDERSTAND."— *Froebel.*

FINGER PLAYS

FOR NURSERY AND KINDERGARTEN

BY
EMILIE POULSSON

Music By
CORNELIA C. ROESKE

Illustrations By L. J. BRIDGMAN

LOTHROP LEE AND SHEPARD CO.

PREFACE.

"WHAT the child imitates," says Froebel, "he begins to understand. Let him represent the flying of birds and he enters partially into the life of birds. Let him imitate the rapid motion of fishes in the water and his sympathy with fishes is quickened. Let him reproduce the activities of farmer, miller and baker, and his eyes open to the meaning of their work. In one word let him reflect in his play the varied aspects of life and his thought will begin to grapple with their significance."

In all times and among all nations, finger-plays have been a delight of childhood Countless babies have laughed and crowed over "Pat-a-cake" and other performances of the soft little hands; while children of whatever age never fail to find amusement in playing

> "Here is the church,
> And here's the steeple,
> Open the doors,
> And here are the people!"

and others as well known.

Yet it is not solely upon the pleasure derived from them, that finger-plays depend for their *raison d'etre*. By their judicious and early use, the development of strength and flexibility in the tiny lax fingers may be assisted, and dormant thought may receive its first awakening call through the motions which interpret as well as illustrate the phase of life or activity presented by the words.

The eighteen finger-plays contained in this book have already, through publication in BABYLAND, been introduced to their especial public, and have been much used in homes, though perhaps more in kindergartens. It will readily be seen that while some of the plays are for the babies in the nursery, others are more suitable for older children.

A baby-friend, ten months old, plays "All for Baby" throughout, pounding and clapping gleefully with all his might — while children seven or eight years of age play and sing "The Caterpillar," "How the Corn Grew" and others with very evident enjoyment

With a little study of the charming and expressive pictures with which the artist, Mr. L. J. Bridgman, has so sympathetically illustrated the rhymes, mothers and kinder gartners have easily understood what motions were intended. To elucidate still farther, however, the playing of " The Merry Little Men " may be thus described :

During the singing of the first verse, the children look about in every direction for the "little men," but keep the hands hidden At the beginning of the second verse, raise both hands to full view with fingers outspread and quiet. At the words, " The first to come," etc., let the thumbs be shown alone, then the others as named in turn, till all are again outspread as at the beginning of the second verse. In the last verse the arms are moved from side to side, hands being raised and fingers fluttering nimbly all the time. When displaying the "busy little men," raise the hands as high as possible.

The music, composed by Miss Cornelia C. Roeske, will be found melodious and attractive and especially suited to the voices and abilities of the very young children for whom it is chiefly intended.

The harmonic arrangement is also purposely simple in consideration of the many mothers and kindergartners who cannot devote time to preparatory practice.

EMILIE POULSSON.

Boston, 1889.

CONTENTS.

DEDICATED
TO
,ITTLE CHILDREN
AT HOME AND IN KINDERGARTEN
BY THEIR FRIEND,
EMILIE POULSSON

I. THE LITTLE MEN.

I. THE LITTLE MEN.

Oh! where are the merry, merry Little Men
  To join us in our play?
And where are the busy, busy Little Men
  To help us work to-day?

MERRY LITTLE MEN

BUSY LITTLE MEN

MASTER THUMB

POINTER

Upon each hand
  A little band
For work or play is ready.
  The first to come
  Is Master Thumb;
Then Pointer, strong and steady;

Then Tall Man high;
And just close by
The Feeble Man doth linger;
And last of all,
So fair and small,
The baby — Little Finger.

Yes! here are the merry, merry Little Men
To join us in our play;
And here are the busy, busy Little Men
To help us work to-day.

THE MERRY LITTLE MEN.

Emilie Poulsson.

Cornelia C. Roeske.

Oh! where are the mer - ry, mer-ry Lit - tle Men To join us in our play? And where are the bus - y, bus - y Lit - tle Men To help us work to-day? Up - on each hand a lit - tle band for work or play is

read - y. The first to come Is Mas - ter Thumb; Then Pointer, strong and stead - y; Then

Tall Man high; And just close by The Fee - ble Man doth lin - ger; And last of all, So

fair and small, The ba - by—Lit - tle Fin - ger. Yes! here are the mer - ry, mer - ry Lit - tle Men To

join us in our play; And here are the bus - y, bus - y Lit - tle Men To help us work to - day.

II. THE LAMBS.

This is the meadow where all the long day
Ten little frolicsome lambs are at play.

THE
MEADOW

These are the measures the good farmer brings
Salt in, or cornmeal, and other good things.

THE
MEASURES

THE
TROUGH

This is the lambkins' own big water-trough;
Drink, little lambkins, and then scamper off!

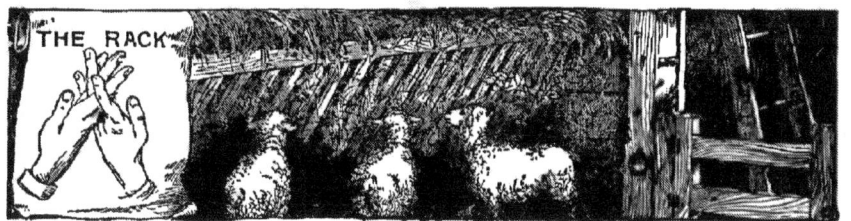

This is the rack where in winter they feed;
Hay makes a very good dinner indeed.

These are the big shears to shear the old sheep;
Dear little lambkins their soft wool may keep.

Here, with its big double doors shut so tight,
This is the barn where they all sleep at night.

THE LAMBS.

Emilie Poulsson   Cornelia C. Roeske.

1. This is the mead-ow where all the long day   Ten lit-tle frol-icsome lambs are at play.

These are the measures the good farmer brings   Salt in, or corn meal, and oth-er good things.

2 This is the lambkins' own big water-trough;
Drink, little lambkins, and then scamper off!
This is the rack where in winter they feed;
Hay makes a very good dinner indeed.

3 These are the big shears to shear the old sheep;
Dear little lambkins their soft wool may keep
Here, with its big double doors shut so tight,
This is the barn where they all sleep at night.

III. THE HEN AND CHICKENS.

III. THE HEN AND CHICKENS.

Good Mother Hen sits here on her nest,
Keeps the eggs warm beneath her soft breast,
  Waiting, waiting, day after day.

ON THE NEST.

BREAKING THE SHELL Hark! there's a sound she knows very well:
  Some little chickens are breaking the shell,
    Pecking, pecking, pecking away.

HAPPY AND PROUD

Now they're all out, Oh, see what a crowd!
Good Mother Hen is happy and proud,
  Cluck-cluck, cluck-cluck, clucking away.

Into the coop the mother must go;
But all the chickens run to and fro,
  Peep-peep, peep-peep, peeping away.

Here is some corn in my little dish;
  Eat, Mother Hen, eat all that you wish,
  Picking, picking, picking away.

Happy we'll be to see you again,
Dear little chicks and good Mother Hen!
Now good-by, good-by for to-day.

THE HEN AND CHICKENS.

EMILIE POULSSON.　　　　　　　　　　　CORNELIA C. ROESKE.

1. Good Moth - er Hen sits here on her nest,
2. Hark! there's a sound she knows ver - y well:
3. Now they're all out, oh, see what a crowd!

Keeps the eggs warm be-neath her soft breast, Wait-ing, wait-ing, day af - ter day.
Some lit - tle chick - ens breaking the shell, Peck - ing, peck-ing, peck - ing a - way.
Good Moth-er Hen is hap - py and proud, Cluck-cluck, cluck-cluck, cluck-ing a - way.

4 Into the coop the mother must go;
While all the chickens run to and fro,
Peep-peep, peep-peep, peeping away.

5 Here is some corn in my little dish;
Eat, Mother Hen, eat all that you wish.
Picking, picking, picking away.

6 Happy we'll be to see you again,
Dear little chicks and good Mother Hen!
Now good-bye, good-bye for to-day.

IV. THE LITTLE PLANT.

IV. THE LITTLE PLANT.

THE BED.

THE RAKE.

SEEDS I SOW.

WITH SOFT EARTH COVER.

In my little garden bed
   Raked so nicely over,
First the tiny seeds I sow,
   Then with soft earth cover.

THE GREAT ROUND SUN.

Shining down, the great round sun
   Smiles upon it often;
Little raindrops, pattering down,
   Help the seeds to soften.

PATTERING

DRUMMING WITH THE FINGER-TIPS.

"DOWN THE ROOTS 'GO"

"LIFTS ITS LITTLE HEAD"

Then the little plant awakes!
  Down the roots go creeping.
Up it lifts its little head
  Through the brown mould peeping.

OPEN INTO FLOWERS

"STILL IT GROWS"

ELEVATING THE ARM AND RAISING THE THUMB FROM THE HAND

High and higher still it grows
  Through the summer hours,
Till some happy day the buds
  Open into flowers.

THE LITTLE PLANT.

Emilie Poulsson.   C. C. Roeske.

1. In my lit - tle garden bed Rak'd so nice - ly o - ver,
2. Then the lit-tle plant awakes! Down the roots go creeping.

First the ti-ny seeds I sow, Then with soft earth cover. Shining down, the great round sun Smiles upon it often;
Up it lifts its little head Thro' the brown mould peeping. High and higher still it grows Thro' the summer hours,

Little raindrops, patt'ring down, Help the seeds to soft-en.
Till some hap-py day the buds O - pen in - to flow-ers.

V. THE PIGS.

V. THE PIGS.

PIGGY WIG

PIGGY WEE

BEHIND THE GATE

Piggie Wig and Piggie Wee,
Hungry pigs as pigs could be,
For their dinner had to wait
Down behind the barnyard gate.

Piggie Wig and Piggie Wee
Climbed the barnyard gate to see,
Peeping through the gate so high,
But no dinner could they spy.

PEEPING
THROUGH

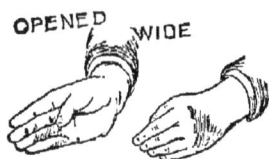

Piggie Wig and Piggie Wee
Got down sad as pigs could be;
But the gate soon opened wide
And they scampered forth outside.

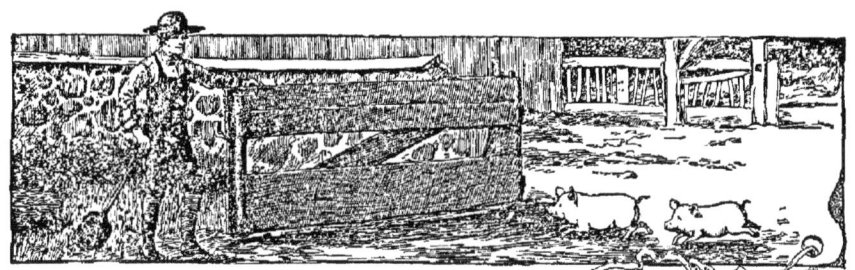

Piggie Wig and Piggie Wee,
What was their delight to see
Dinner ready not far off —
Such a full and tempting trough!

Piggie Wig and Piggie Wee,
Greedy pigs as pigs could be,
For their dinner ran pell-mell;
In the trough both piggies fell.

THE PIGS.

EMILIE POULSSON. CORNELIA O. ROESKE.

1. Pig-gie Wig and Pig-gie Wee,

Hun-gry pigs as pigs could be, For their din-ner had to wait Down behind the barn-yard gate.

2 Piggie Wig and Piggie Wee
  Climbed the barn-yard gate to see,
  Peeping through the gate so high,
  But no dinner could they spy.

3 Piggie Wig and Piggie Wee
  Got down sad as pigs could be;
  But the gate soon opened wide
  And they scampered forth outside.

4 Piggie Wig and Piggie Wee,
  What was their delight to see
  Dinner ready not far off —
  Such a full and tempting trough!

5 Piggie Wig and Piggie Wee,
  Greedy pigs as pigs could be,
  For their dinner ran pell-mell;
  In the trough both piggies fell.

VI. 'A LITTLE BOY'S WALK.

VI. A LITTLE BOY'S WALK.

THE RABBIT

RAN AWAY

THE FISHES

A little boy went. walking
    One lovely summer's day:
He saw a little rabbit
    That quickly ran away;

He saw a shining river
    Go winding in and out,
And little fishes in it
    Were swimming all about;

SHINING RIVER

CHURCH STEEPLE

MILL WHEEL

And, slowly, slowly turning,
    The great wheel of the mill;
And then the tall church steeple,
    The little church so still;

The bridge above the water;
  And when he stopped to rest,
He saw among the bushes
  A wee ground-sparrow's nest.

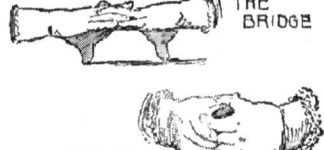

And as he watched the birdies
  Above the tree-tops fly,
He saw the clouds a-sailing
  Across the sunny sky.

He saw the insects playing;
  The flowers that summer brings;
He said, "I'll go tell mamma!
  I've seen *so many* things!"

A LITTLE BOY'S WALK.

Emilie Poulsson.   Cornelia C. Roesen.

A lit-tle boy went walk-ing One lovely summer's day: He saw a lit-tle rab-bit That quickly ran a-way; He saw a shin-ing riv-er Go wind-ing in and out, And lit-tle fish-es in it Were swimming all a-bout.

And slow-ly, slow-ly turn-ing, The great wheel of the mill; And then the tall church steeple, The little church so still; The bridge above the wa-ter; And when he stopped to rest, He saw among the bush-es A wee ground-sparrow's nest

And as he watched the bird-ies A-bove the tree-tops fly, He saw the clouds a-sail-ing A-cross the sun-ny sky, He saw the in-sects play-ing; The flowers that summer brings; He said, "I'll go tell Mamma I've seen so man-y things."

VII. THE CATERPILLAR.

VII. THE CATERPILLAR.

CRAWLING
Move whole hand forward
and wriggle the thumb.

NOWHERE TO BE FOUND

Fuzzy little caterpillar,
Crawling, crawling on the ground!
Fuzzy little caterpillar,
Nowhere, nowhere to be found,
Though we've looked and looked and hunted
Everywhere around!

When the little caterpillar
Found his furry coat too tight,
Then a snug cocoon he made him
Spun of silk so soft and light;
Rolled himself away within it—
Slept there day and night.

ROLLED
HIMSELF
AWAY

(Rotate
the thumb,
then double
into the
hand.)

STIRRING

A HEAD WE SPY

See how this cocoon is stirring!
Now a little head we spy—
What! Is *this* our caterpillar
Spreading gorgeous wings to dry?
Soon the free and happy creature
Flutters gayly by.

SPREADING
GORGEOUS
WINGS

FLUTTERS (Move palms to and fro)

Bridgman

THE CATERPILLAR.

Emilie Poulsson.

Cornelia C. Roeske.

1. Fuz - zy lit - tle cat - er - pil - lar, Crawling, crawling
2. When the lit - tle cat - er - pil - lar Found his fur - ry
3. See how this co - coon is stir - ring! Now a lit - tle

on the ground! Fuz - zy lit - tle cat - er - pil - lar, Nowhere, nowhere to be found, Tho' we've looked and
coat too tight, Then a snug co-coon he made him Spun of silk so soft and light; Rolled himself a -
head we spy—What! is *this* our cat - er - pil - lar Spreading gorgeous wings to dry? Soon the free and

looked and hunted Ev - erywhere a - round!
way with-in it—Slept there day and night.
hap - py crea-ture Flut-ters gai - ly by.

VIII. ALL FOR BABY.

VIII. ALL FOR BABY.

Here's a ball for Baby,
Big and soft and round!
Here is Baby's hammer —
O, how he can pound!

Here is Baby's music —
Clapping, clapping so!
Here are Baby's soldiers,
Standing in a row!

Here's the Baby's trumpet,
Toot-too-toot! too-too!
Here's the way that **Baby**
Plays at " Peep-a-boo! "

Here's a big umbrella —
Keep the Baby dry!
Here's the Baby's cradle —
Rock-a-baby-by!

ALL FOR BABY.

Emilie Poulsson.   Cornelia C. Roeske.

1. Here's a ball for Ba - by, Big and soft and round! Here is Ba - by's ham-mer —

O, how he can pound!

2 Here is Baby's music
   Clapping, clapping so!
   Here are Baby's soldiers,
   Standing in a row !

3 Here's the Baby's trumpet,
   Toot-too-toot! too-too!
   Here's the way that Baby
   Plays at "Peep-a-boo!"

4 Here's a big umbrella —
   Keeps the Baby dry!
   Here's the Baby's cradle —
   Rock-a-baby by!

IX. THE MICE.

IX. THE MICE.

Five little mice on the pantry floor,
Seeking for bread-crumbs or something more;

Five little mice on the shelf up high,
Feasting so daintily on a pie —

But the big round eyes of the wise old cat
See what the five little mice are at.

Quickly she jumps!—but the mice run away,
And hide in their snug little holes all day.

"Feasting in pantries may be very nice;
But home is the best!" say the five little mice.

"MICE
RUN
AWAY"

Left hand lowered
suddenly [Pounce of the
cat] Right hand
brought behind the
back [Mice run away]

HOME

FIVE LITTLE MICE.

Emilie Poulsson.   Cornelia C. Roeske.

1. { Five lit-tle mice on the pan-try floor,
{ big round eyes of the wise old cat

Seeking for bread crumbs or something more; Five little mice on the shelf up high,
See what the five lit-tle mice are at. Quick-ly she jumps! but the mice run a-way, And

1

D.S.

Feast-ing so dain-ti-ly on a pie —
hide in their snug lit-tle holes all day.

But the

2

"Feasting in pan-tries may be ver-y nice; But home is the best!" say the five lit-tle mice.

X. THE SQUIRREL.

X. THE SQUIRREL.

IN THE HOLLOW TREE

THE CAGE

"Little squirrel, living there
In the hollow tree,
I've a pretty cage for you;
Come and live with me!

"You may turn the little wheel—
That will be great fun!
Slowly round, or very fast
If you faster run.

THE WHEEL

"Little squirrel, I will bring
In my basket here
Every day a feast of nuts!
Come, then, squirrel dear."

But the little squirrel said
From his hollow tree:
"Oh! no, no! I'd rather far
Live here and be free!"

So my cage is empty yet,
And the wheel is still;
But my little basket here
Oft with nuts I fill.

If you like, I'll crack the nuts,
Some for you and me,
For the squirrel has enough
In his hollow tree.

THE SQUIRREL.

Emilie Poulsson.   Cornelia C. Roeske.

1. "Lit-tle Squirrel, liv-ing there In the hol-low
2. "Lit-tle Squirrel, I will bring In my bas-ket
3. So my cage is emp-ty yet And the wheel is

tree, I've a pret-ty cage for you; Come and live with me! You may turn the
here Ev-ery day a feast of nuts! Come then, squir-rel dear." But the lit-tle
still; But my lit-tle bas-ket here Oft with nuts I fill. If you like, I'll

lit-tle wheel—That will be great fun! Slow-ly round, or ver-y fast If you fast-er run."
squir-rel said From his hol-low tree: "Oh! no, no! I'd rath-er far Live here and be free."
crack the nuts, Some for you and me, For the squir-rel has enough In his hol-low tree.

XI. THE SPARROWS.

XI. THE SPARROWS.

"Little brown sparrows,
Flying around,
Up in the tree-tops,
Down on the ground,

"Come to my window,
Dear sparrows, come!
See! I will give you
Many a crumb.

"Here is some water,
Sparkling and clear;
Come, little sparrows,
Drink without fear.

"If you are tired,
Here is a nest;
Wouldn't you like to
Come here to rest?"

All the brown sparrows
Flutter away,
Chirping and singing,
"We cannot stay;

"For in the tree-tops,
'Mong the gray boughs,
There is the sparrows'
Snug little house."

SOME WATER

A NEST

THE HOUSE

FLY AWAY
Raise Hands
Fluttering Fingers

THE SPARROWS.

Emilie Poulsson.   C. C. Roeske.

1. "Lit - tle brown spar - rows, Fly - ing a - round,   Up in the tree - tops,
2. "Here is some wa - ter, Spark-ling and clear;   Come, lit - tle spar - rows,
3 All the brown spar - rows Flut - ter a - way,   Chirp-ing and sing - ing,

Down on the ground,   Come to my window, Dear spar - rows, come!
Drink with-out fear.   If you are tired,   Here is a nest;
"We can - not stay;   For in the tree - tops, 'Mong the gray boughs,

See! I will give you Man-y a crumb."
Wouldn't you like to Come here and rest?"
There is the spar - rows' Snug lit-tle house."

XII. THE COUNTING LESSON.

XII. THE COUNTING LESSON.

(*Right hand.*)

Here is the beehive. Where are the bees?
Hidden away where nobody sees.
Soon they come creeping out of the hive —
One! — two! — three! four! five!

(*Left hand.*)

Once I saw an ant-hill
  With no ants about;
So I said, "Dear little ants,
  Won't you please come out?"
Then as if the little ants
  Had heard my call —
One! two! three! four! *five* came out!
  And that was all!

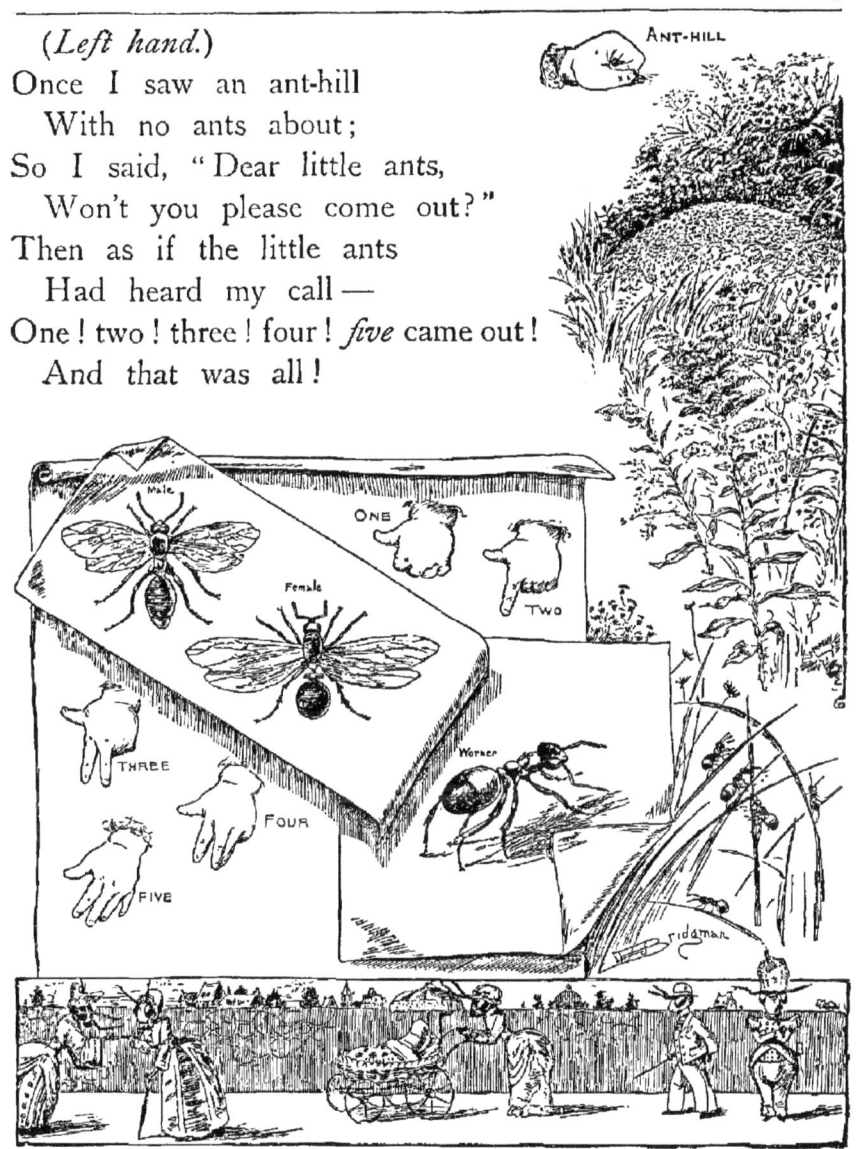

THE COUNTING LESSON.

Emilie Poulsson.

C. C. Roeske.

1ST VERSE.

1. Here is the beehive. Where are the bees? Hid-den a - way where no-bod-y sees.

Soon they come creep-ing out of the hive — One! — two! — three! four! five!

2ND VERSE.

2. Once I saw an ant hill With no ants a - bout; So I said,

"Dear lit-tle ants, Won't you please come out?" Then as if the lit - tle ants Had

heard my call — One! two! three! four! five came out! And that was all!

XIII. MRS. PUSSY'S DINNER.

XIII. MRS. PUSSY'S DINNER.

Mrs. Pussy, sleek and fat,
With her kittens four,
Went to sleep upon the mat
By the kitchen door.

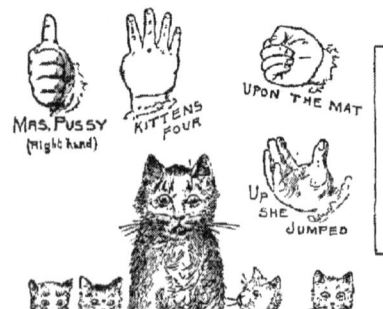

Mrs. Pussy heard a noise —
Up she jumped in glee:
"Kittens, maybe that's a mouse!
Let us go and see!"

Creeping, creeping, creeping on,
Silently they stole;
But the little mouse had gone
Back within its hole.

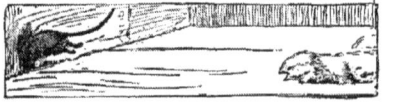

"Well," said Mrs. Pussy then,
"To the barn we'll go;
We shall find the swallow there
Flying to and fro."

So the cat and kittens four
Tried their very best;
But the swallows flying fast
Safely reached the nest!

Home went hungry Mrs. Puss
And her kittens four;
Found their dinner on a plate
By the kitchen door.

Mrs. Puss said, "Meow! To chase
Birds and mice is fun;
But I'm glad that dinner-plates
Cannot fly or run!"

1. Mrs. Pus-sy, sleek and fat, With her kittens four,

Went to sleep up - on the mat By the kitchen door.

2 Mrs. Pussy heard a noise —
  Up she jumped in glee:
  "Kittens, maybe that's a mouse!
  Let us go and see!"

3 Creeping, creeping, creeping on,
  Silently they stole;
  But the little mouse had gone
  Back within its hole.

4 "Well," said Mrs. Pussy then,
  "To the barn we'll go;
  We shall find the swallows there
  Flying to and fro."

5 So the cat and kittens four
  Tried their very best;
  But the swallows flying fast
  Safely reached the nest!

6 Home went hungry Mrs. Puss
  And her kittens four;
  Found their dinner on a plate
  By the kitchen door.

7 Mrs. Puss said, "Meow! To chase
  Birds and mice is fun;
  But I'm glad that dinner-plates
  Cannot fly or run!"

XIV. HOW THE CORN GREW.

XIV. How The Corn Grew.

There was a field that waiting lay,
  All hard and brown and bare;
There was a thrifty farmer came
  And fenced it in with care.

THE FIELD

THE HARROW

THE PLOW

Then came a plowman with his plow;
  From early until late,
Across the field and back again,
  He plowed the furrows straight.

The harrow then was brought to make
  The ground more soft and loose;
And soon the farmer said with joy,
  " My field is fit for use."

For many days the farmer then
   Was working with his hoe;
And little Johnny brought the corn
   And dropped the kernels — so!

And there they lay, until awaked
   By tapping rains that fell,
Then pushed their green plumes up
     to greet
The sun they loved so well.

THE HOE

DROPPED THE KERNELS —SO!

"POKED THEIR GREEN PLUMES UP

THE GUN (Snap the fingers)

TAPPING RAINS (Drumming with the fingers)

THE SICKLE

Then flocks and flocks of hungry crows
   Came down the corn to taste;
But ba-ang! — went the farmer's gun
   And off they flew in haste.

Then grew and grew the corn, until,
   When autumn days had come,
With sickles keen they cut it down,
   And sang the "Harvest Home."

HOW THE CORN GREW.

Emilie Poulsson.

Cornelia C. Roeske.

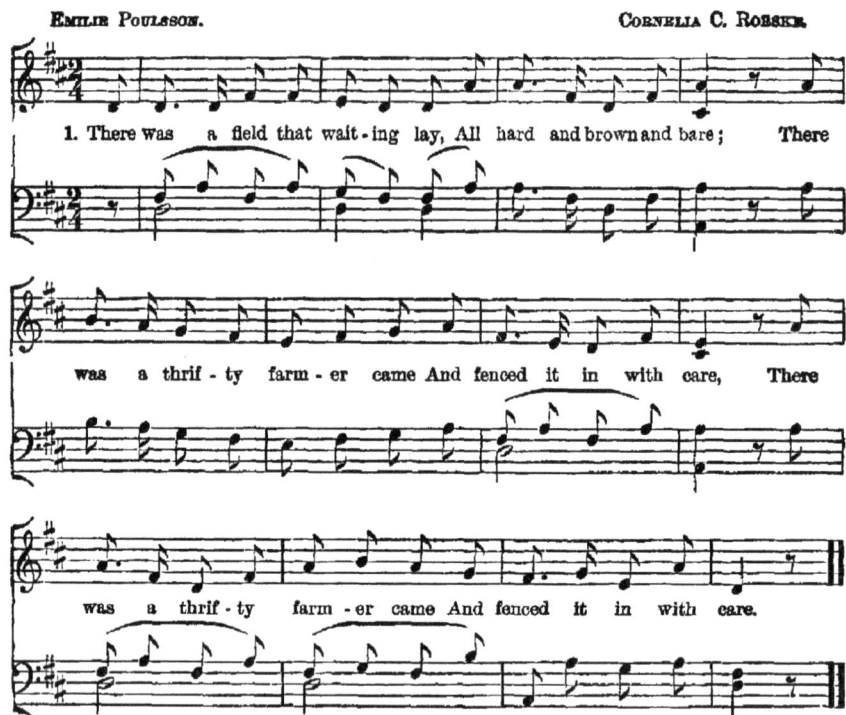

1. There was a field that wait-ing lay, All hard and brown and bare; There
was a thrif-ty farm-er came And fenced it in with care, There
was a thrif-ty farm-er came And fenced it in with care.

2 Then came a ploughman with his plough;
From early until late,
Across the field and back again,
He ploughed the furrows straight.

3 The harrow then was brought to make
The ground more soft and loose;
And soon the farmer said with joy,
"My field is fit for use."

4 For many days the farmer then
Was working with his hoe;
And little Johnny brought the corn
And dropped the kernels — so!

5 And there they lay, until awaked
By tapping rains that fell,
Then pushed their green plumes up to greet
The sun they loved so well.

6 Then flocks and flocks of hungry crows
Came down the corn to taste;
But ba-ang! went the farmer's gun,
And off they flew in haste.

7 Then grew and grew the corn, until,
When autumn days had come,
With sickles keen they cut it down,
And sang the "Harvest Home."

XV. THE MILL.

XV. THE MILL.

THE MILLDAM

A merry little river
  Went singing day by day,
Until it reached a mill-dam
  That stretched across its way.

And there it spread its waters,
  A quiet pond, to wait
Until the busy miller
  Should lift the water-gate.

Then, hurrying through the gateway,
  The dashing waters found
A mighty millwheel waiting,
  And turned it swiftly round.

LIFT THE WATER-GATE

THE MILLWHEEL

But faster turned the millstones
  Up in the dusty mill,
And quickly did the miller
  With corn the hopper fill.

And faster yet and faster
  The heavy stones went round,
Until the golden kernels
  To golden meal were ground.

" Now fill the empty hopper
  With *wheat*," the miller said ;
"We'll grind this into flour
  To make the children's bread."

THE
MILLSTONES

THE
HOPPER

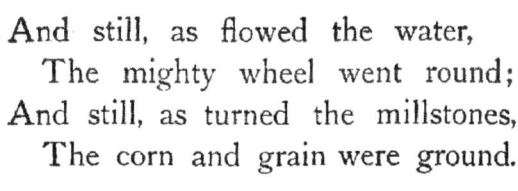

And still, as flowed the water,
  The mighty wheel went round;
And still, as turned the millstones,
  The corn and grain were ground.

And busy was the miller
  The livelong day, until
The water-gate he fastened,
  And silent grew the mill.

THE MILL.

EMILIE POULSSON.

CORNELIA C. ROESKE.

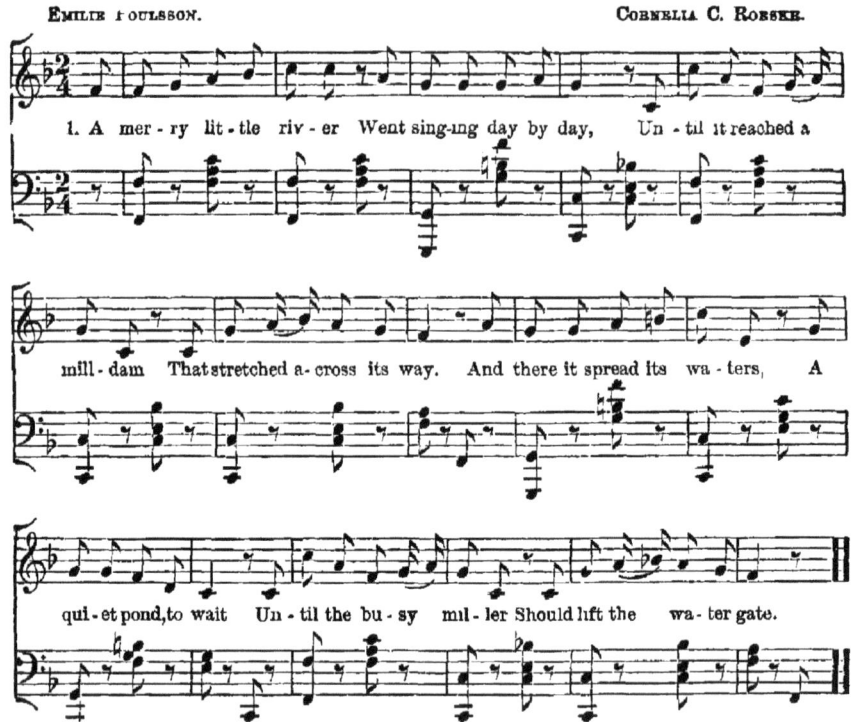

1. A mer-ry lit-tle riv-er Went sing-ing day by day, Un-til it reached a mill-dam That stretched a-cross its way. And there it spread its wa-ters, A qui-et pond, to wait Un-til the bu-sy mil-ler Should lift the wa-ter gate.

2 Then, hurrying through the gateway,
  The dashing waters found
A mighty millwheel waiting—
  And turned it swiftly round.
But faster turned the millstone
  Up in the dusty mill,
And quickly did the miller
  With corn the hopper fill.

3 And faster yet and faster
  The heavy stones went round,
Until the golden kernels
  To golden meal were ground.

"Now, fill the empty hopper
  With *wheat*," the miller said;
" We'll grind this into flour
  To make the children's bread."

4 And still, as flowed the water,
  The mighty wheel went round;
And still, as turned the millstones,
  The corn and grain were ground.
And busy was the miller
  The livelong day, until
The water gate he fastened,
  And silent grew the mill.

XVI. MAKING BREAD.

XVI. MAKING BREAD.

"The farmer and the miller
Have worked," the mother said,
"And got the flour ready,
So I will make the bread."
She scooped from out the barrel
The flour white as snow,
And in her sieve she put it
And shook it to and fro.

Then in the pan of flour
A little salt she threw;
A cup of yeast she added,
And poured in water, too.
To mix them all together
She stirred with busy might,
Then covered it and left it
Until the bread was light.

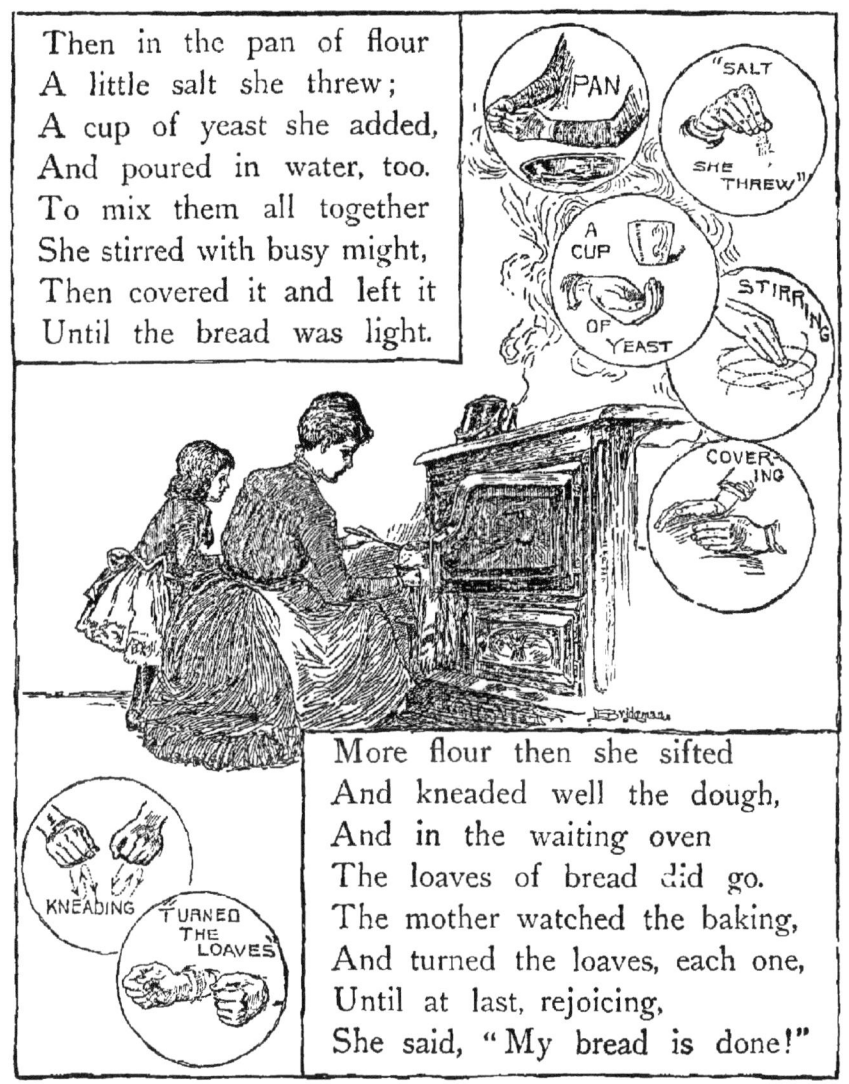

More flour then she sifted
And kneaded well the dough,
And in the waiting oven
The loaves of bread did go.
The mother watched the baking,
And turned the loaves, each one,
Until at last, rejoicing,
She said, "My bread is done!"

MAKING BREAD.

Emilie Poulsson.

C. C. Roeske.

1. "The farm-er and the mil-ler Have work'd,"the mother said, "And got the flo-ur read-y, So I will make the bread." She scooped from out the bar-rel The flo-ur white as snow, And in her sieve she put it And shook it to and fro.

2 Then in the pan of flour
  A little salt she threw;
A cup of yeast she added,
  And poured in water, too.
To mix them all together
  She stirred with busy might,
Then covered it and left it
  Until the bread was light.

3 More flour then she sifted
  And kneaded well the dough,
And in the waiting oven
  The loaves of bread did go.
The mother watched the baking,
  And turned the loaves, each one
Until at last, rejoicing,
  She said, " My bread is done! "

XVII. MAKING BUTTER.

XVII. MAKING BUTTER.

SKIMMER

CHURNING

Skim, skim, skim,
  With the skimmer bright;
Take the rich and yellow cream,
  Leave the milk so white.

Churn, churn, churn,
  Now 'tis churning day;
Till the cream to butter turn
  Dasher must not stay.

Press, press, press;
  All the milk must be
From the golden butter now
  Pressed out carefully

BOWL

LADLE
(for pressing)

A ROLL
OF
BUTTER

"PAT, PAT, PAT"

SPREADING

Pat, pat, pat;
  Make it smooth and round.
See! the roll of butter's done —
  Won't you buy a pound?

Taste, oh! taste,
  This is very nice;
Spread it on the children's bread,
  Give them each a slice.

MAKING BUTTER.

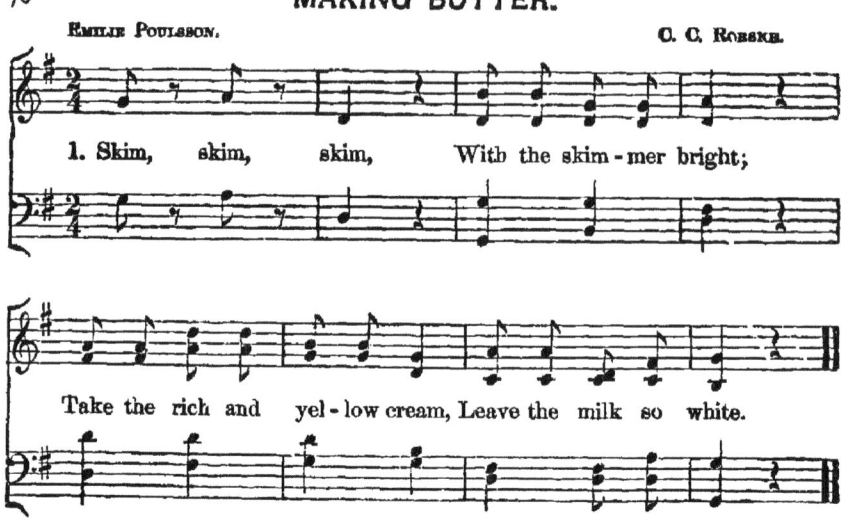

EMILIE POULSSON.

C. C. ROESKE.

1. Skim, skim, skim, With the skim-mer bright;

Take the rich and yel-low cream, Leave the milk so white.

2 Churn, churn, churn,
    Now 'tis churning day;
  Till the cream to butter turn
    Dasher must not stay.

3 Press, press, press;
    All the milk must be
  From the golden butter now
    Pressed out carefully.

4 Pat, pat, pat,
    Make it smooth and round.
  See! the roll of butter's done —
    Won't you buy a pound?

5 Taste, oh! taste,
    This is very nice.
  Spread it on the children's bread,
    Give them each a slice.

XVIII. SANTA CLAUS.

XVIII. SANTA CLAUS.

O, clap, clap the hands,
  And sing out with glee!
For Christmas is coming
  And merry are we!

PAIR OF REINDEER

IN SECOND AND FOURTH VERSES

CLAPPING

THROUGH THE FIRST AND LAST VERSES

Now swift o'er the snow
  The tiny reindeer
Are trotting and bringing
  Good Santa Claus near.

Our stockings we'll hang,
    And while we're asleep
Then down through the chimney
    Will Santa Claus creep

He'll empty his pack,
    Then up he will come
And, calling his reindeer,
    Will haste away home.

STOCKINGS

SANTA CLAUS

DOWN THE CHIMNEY

UP HE WILL COME

Then clap, clap the hands!
    And sing out with glee,
For Christmas is coming
    And merry are we!

SANTA CLAUS.

EMILIE POULSSON.   CORNELIA C. ROESKE.

1. O, clap, clap the hands, And sing out with glee! For
2. O, clap, clap the hands, And sing out with glee! For
3. O, clap, clap the hands, And sing out with glee! For

Christ-mas is com-ing and mer-ry are we! Now swift o'er the snow The
Christ-mas is com-ing and mer-ry are we! Our stock-ings we'll hang, And
Christ-mas is com-ing and mer-ry are we! He'll emp-ty his pack, Then

ti-ny rein-deer Are trot-ting and bring-ing Good San-ta Claus near.
while we're a-sleep Then down thro' the chim-ney Will San-ta Claus creep.
up he will come And, call-ing the rein-deer, Will haste a-way home.

Milton Keynes UK
Ingram Content Group UK Ltd.
UKHW022027110124
435898UK00005B/93